⚜

EX LIBRIS

May this book
give you the secrets
to bring God's blessings
into your life -
Pat Robertson

THE
GREATEST
VIRTUE

PAT ROBERTSON

THE GREATEST VIRTUE

CBN

Virginia Beach, VA

Product Number 00950

Printed in the United States of America

07 08 09 10   RRD   5 4 3 2 1

Humble yourselves before the Lord,
and he will lift you up in honor.

JAMES 4:10 NLT

An humble able man is a jewel worth a kingdom.
WILLIAM PENN

CONTENTS

FOREWORD

At no time in the turbulent sea of American history was there a greater need than now to rediscover the blessed waters of humility. This is true for religious and secular alike. Simply stated, without humility America will not long endure. Pride has eaten alive every other nation that has preceded us.

The same is true for religion in America. Humility is the only true barometer of religious authenticity because it is the direct consequence of a true proximity with G-d.[1] In the face of a perfect being, we discover our own imperfection. In the face of an omniscient being we discover our own ignorance. And in the face of an infinitely loving Creator, we discover our much more limited hearts.

As a nation we must chart not our own arrogant path but learn, as the prophet Micah said, "to walk humbly"[2] with our G-d.

I have had the great pleasure of spending many hours discussing humility with the Reverend Pat Robertson where both our understandings of this most central issue of faith was deepened and enriched. His book on the subject is a gift, illuminating beautifully what humility is and its application to a more spiritual and purposeful life.

As a Jew, I humbly offer my thanks to my friend Pat for his untiring devotion to the survival and flourishing of Israel against many arrogant enemies who falsely believe that religion is about hatred rather than harmony and about belligerence rather than brotherhood.

This book will serve as a treasure for those who wish to bring the bountiful blessing of humility into their everyday lives.

May a loving G-d bless you all.

RABBI SHMULEY BOTEACH

CHAIRMAN, JEWISH VALUES NETWORK,
AND HOST OF THE LEARNING CHANNEL'S
SHALOM IN THE HOME

WARS OF PRIDE

Unless humility precede, accompany, and follow up all the good we accomplish, unless we keep our eyes fixed on it, pride will snatch everything right out of our hands.

SAINT AUGUSTINE OF HIPPO

Bitter rumors and confusion are now the hallmarks of United States politics as a president from the Republican Party lurches back and forth in battle with a Congress controlled by members of the Democratic Party. The political struggle centers around an ill-conceived war in Iraq that may be unwinnable and yet will ultimately cost the United States taxpayers the incredible sum of $1 trillion, not to mention the shattered lives and bodies of at least thirty thousand brave servicemen and servicewomen.

This is a book about humility, and what does humility have to do with the Second Iraq War, in fact, all wars? The answer: everything!

In truth, with few exceptions, the aggressive wars of mankind's existence are brought about by the selfish pride of kings, generals, chieftains, tribes, and clans. Think for a moment about the excesses of Hitler's Germany.

The Germans were told that they belonged to the Aryan or master race. Then they were told that they deserved *lebensraum*, or living space. Then they were told that their nation under the Nazis, the Third Reich, would exist for a thousand years and would replace the millennium of peace promised in the Bible. Along the way, they were told that their leader deserved god-like reverence and obedience. In his pride, Adolf Hitler portrayed himself as the embodiment of all the national hopes and aspirations of the German people.

The entire apparatus of government became a vehicle to exalt Hitler and his Nazi followers. The parades, the flags, the mass meetings, the polished jackboots, the propaganda movies, the martial music, the patriotic appeals—all built to the crescendo of war against the Poles, the Czechs, the Belgians, the Danes, the Dutch, the French, and then the Russians—all to satisfy the sickening pride of one man and his slavish followers.

Pride brought about the Holocaust of terror against the Jews of Europe—banishment and expropriation, hideous torture, starvation, and the tragic death of six million victims. From the rise of Hitler and the Nazis until the end of World War II, pride and arrogance had claimed the lives of fifty million warriors and civilians.

Alexander of Macedonia was one of the most brilliant generals in history. Perhaps he began with a belief that he was defending Macedonia against Persia. But that belief quickly changed until he was so consumed with personal pride and vainglory that, having swept away the empires of antiquity, he wept at the Indus River in what is now Pakistan because he had no more worlds to conquer.

Rome began as a small city with noble and democratic ideals that commended itself to adjoining regions of Italy because of its laws, its culture, its scientific achievements, and its business success. That humble concept soon degenerated into a military colossus intent on subjugating the known world—no longer a republic, but an empire ruled by a succession of increasingly prideful emperors who at last declared that they were gods worthy of worship.

The entire apparatus of government became a vehicle to exalt Hitler and his Nazi followers.

When we think of Alexander, Caesar, Napoleon, Hitler, Stalin, Mao Tse-tung, the pharaohs, the czars of Russia, and the kings of Spain, France, and England, the word *humble* never comes to mind. *Arrogant, prideful, vainglorious, ruthless*—but never *humble*.

Returning our attention to the Iraq War, which has so tragically divided the people of the United States, here is the problem. A small group of policymakers in the Bush administration had convinced themselves that Saddam Hussein was a threat to the Middle East, Israel, and ultimately the United States. They believed that the Iraqi people were chafing under Saddam's ruthless regime and would, therefore, welcome an invading United States Army. Despite the considered judgment of senior military officers, they determined that the mission could be accomplished by a small force of 165,000 men instead of the 500,000 recommended by senior generals.

The arrogant person will reject evidence contrary to his predetermined point of view, but will eagerly seek out anything that supports the opinion already held.

Pride and arrogance tell us that we know better than the experts. Consequently, the arrogant person will reject evidence contrary to his predetermined point of view, but will eagerly seek out anything that supports the opinion already held.

However, it is clear that the opinion of a few policymakers is not adequate to send a huge democracy into a war of aggression. So a massive selling job was required to convince the Congress and the American people that Saddam Hussein had weapons that would not only imperil his neighbors, but the United States as well. We were told repeatedly that "Saddam possessed weapons of mass destruction" (WMDs for short). The most awful weapon of mass destruction is the atomic bomb. In a presidential State of the Union address to Congress, the American people were told that British intelligence had secretly learned that Saddam was negotiating the importation of a material used in atomic bombs, uranium yellowcake, from the African nation of Niger.

The fruit of this bit of arrogant deception was indeed poisonous. Joe Wilson, the government agent sent to verify the claim, reported quite publicly that no yellowcake from Niger had been contracted by Saddam. Humility says, "I was mistaken." Pride attempts to destroy the messenger bringing contrary news.

Before the yellowcake drama played out, a federal prosecutor spent three years of fruitless inquiry into attempts by key figures in the administration to discredit the messenger and his wife, a CIA operative. In the process, a *New York Times* reporter was imprisoned for failure to disclose sources, and a distinguished government lawyer was convicted of lying. To this day, pride and arrogance have prevented the president and his top aides from admitting the inaccuracy of their initial claims.

There is, however, a far more convincing proof of the absence of nuclear devices in Saddam's arsenal. Long before the war, an Iraqi nuclear physicist, Dr. Khidhir Hamza, was commissioned by Saddam to create an Iraqi thermonuclear device. In an excellent book titled *Saddam's Bombmaker*, Dr. Hamza spelled out in clear detail that Saddam did not have nuclear capability, and, given the state of Iraqi science, he would never be able (at least for several decades) to build the centrifuges and cascades to enrich the uranium needed to build a working bomb.

To this day, pride and arrogance have prevented the president and his top aides from admitting the inaccuracy of their initial claims.

I had the pleasure not only of reading Dr. Hamza's book, but of interviewing him twice on my television program, *The 700 Club*. I believed that Dr. Hamza was telling the truth—there were no nukes in Iran. In short, yellowcake was totally irrelevant to a country lacking the scientific prowess and complex technical equipment required to enrich it.

If I, a religious broadcaster, knew this, surely the CIA and other branches of United States intelligence knew what I knew and much more. Surely they relayed this vital intelligence to the president and the vice president. Humility would have demanded that our leaders accept clear-cut truths and alter policy accordingly. But no. Arrogance said, "We know Saddam has WMDs, and we altered the facts to fit our preconceptions." So, like obedient servants, the intelligence agencies began serving up outlandish and bogus claims from dubious sources to support the presuppositions of the political leaders of the United States government.

The intelligence agencies began serving up outlandish and bogus claims from dubious sources to support the presuppositions of the political leaders of the United States government.

The result was a vast propaganda campaign based on unproved assumptions that led the greatest nation on earth into a series of blunders. Those blunders placed us in the middle of a bitter sectarian civil war being waged by centuries-old enemies. The grievances of these enemies are against one another, and Americans cannot hope to understand them fully.

Humility would have urged a careful marshaling of

all known facts, followed by the exercise of extreme caution. Pride and arrogance declared Saddam an international outlaw to be captured and brought to justice regardless of the cost. Only history will reveal the damage this latter course of action will ultimately bring upon this nation.

It is plain to see that although humility is a spiritual virtue extolled by religious thinkers of many faiths, the absence of this virtue can bring untold suffering and tragedy to individuals, families, businesses, and nations.

CHAPTER 2

CORRUPTED BY BEAUTY

The source of humility is the habit of realizing the presence of God.

WILLIAM TEMPLE

The pages of the Holy Bible—from the books of Moses, the Psalms, the Proverbs, and the ancient Hebrew prophets through the Gospels and apostolic letters to the book of Revelation—portray the vast cosmic drama of creation, rebellion, new creation, new rebellion, redemption, and final glorious triumph.

Here is the story . . .

In the beginning, almighty God, a spiritual being wiser, more loving, and more powerful than mere human beings can comprehend, created the material universe. With it, He created a multitude of spiritual beings of great power and beauty known as angels or messengers.

The most exalted angel was known as Lucifer, the "light one." The prophets Isaiah and Ezekiel in their inspired writings transcended discussion of the earthly rulers of Babylon and Tyre to what is a clear indictment of Lucifer's rebellion against God.

Here is how Isaiah described his fall: "How you are fallen from heaven, O Lucifer, son of the morning! How you are cut down to the ground, you who weakened the nations! For you have said in your heart: 'I will ascend into heaven, I will exalt my throne above the stars of God; I will also sit on the mount of the congregation on the farthest sides of the north; I will ascend above the heights of the clouds, I will be like the Most High.'"[1]

Pride above all else is the root sin; in fact, pride is the origin of all sin.

The prophet Ezekiel put it this way: "You were in Eden, the garden of God. . . . You were an anointed guardian cherub. I placed you; you were on the holy mountain of God; in the midst of the stones of fire you walked. You were blameless in your ways from the day you were created, till unrighteousness was found in you. . . . Your heart was proud because of your beauty; you corrupted your wisdom for the sake of your splendor"[2]

A perfect creation. Order, harmony, beauty, and peace. Wisdom and love flowed from a benevolent Creator. All creatures were living in indescribable happiness.

Then Lucifer began to contemplate his beauty, his strength, and his wisdom. He began to be proud because of the very gifts that had been given him by God.

The splendor of his exalted position and his favored access to the Creator overwhelmed his wisdom. In his deluded state, he began to believe that he could ascend above the stars and be like the Most High. He actually believed that he could manage the affairs of the entire universe as capably as the One who had created him. Over and over again, the phrase "I will" comes forth.

Pride above all else is the root sin; in fact, pride is the origin of all sin. Pride says, "I can manage my affairs and every aspect of life more capably than God. I can do it my way, and my way is better than God's way."

Yet we see that the fruit of pride is not a better world; rather, the fruit of pride is murder, hatred, warfare, poverty, and disease. We understand the danger of a world organized by malicious followers of Lucifer. But I pose this question: Does history show any success and betterment from the so-called utopian experiments of people who were convinced they could do a better job than God in ordering society?

A prideful mind-set was painfully evident at the drafting of an organizing statement of the European Community. This region, which once was called Christendom, now, over the strong protest of the

Catholic Church, has refused to make any mention of God in its proclamation celebrating its fiftieth anniversary, and it has refused to acknowledge the clear Christian presence throughout Europe's history. This action was considered so egregious that Pope Benedict declared it a form of "apostasy of itself" and an expression of doubt of its own identity. The pope, who, like his predecessor John Paul, often calls for a mention of God and Christianity in the European Constitution, said leaders could not exclude values that helped forge the "very soul" of the Continent.

In a region where the absence of strong religious faith is leading to a drastically declining birthrate and a resulting long-range demographic disaster, the leaders are too prideful to acknowledge their problem and their need for God's help.

Closer to home, pride (or what is often called *hubris*) has led to the decline of the domestic United States automobile industry. Thirty years ago, the "Big Two" automobile manufacturers, General Motors and Ford, dominated the domestic United States automobile market. Both were hugely profitable. Their stock and bonds were investment grade. Then something happened.

Japanese auto manufacturer Toyota began a novel system of production. Instead of workers taking orders from proud bosses who "knew it all," the workers were formed into small groups to give suggestions on every phase of manufacturing, from overall design to the method of tightening lug nuts. The managers humbled themselves and became "servant leaders." The workers felt empowered to make improvements in Toyota cars, while all concerned humbled themselves to listen to the voices of their customers and to design cars to accommodate the wishes of the men and women who actually purchased automobiles.

Pride (or what is often called hubris) has led to the decline of the domestic United States automobile industry.

In Detroit, the proud captains of industry scoffed at Japan and its fledgling attempts to build cars. After all, the Detroit executives had grown up as pioneers in the industry. They knew, or so they thought, that no one understood as much as they did about building and selling cars. They knew what the market wanted. They knew what had always sold. And they certainly knew more about the mass production of automobiles than the thousands of workers who manned the assembly lines. In short, they were filled with pride, and in their own eyes they were far superior to the little guys from Japan—a nation still recovering from a devastating defeat in World War II.

A prideful mind-set was painfully evident at the drafting of an organizing statement of the European Community.

Because the Japanese workers had been empowered to insist on quality at each step of production, the Toyota cars began to roll off the assembly line relatively defect-free. The finance executives in Detroit determined that excessive quality control was a waste of money. They decreed that automobiles with defects would be sold under a warranty that allowed disgruntled purchasers to bring them back for repair at no charge.

The Japanese humbled themselves to listen to the markets. They began to roll out sleek and smaller fuel-efficient cars with a reputation for superb quality. The proud executives in Detroit continued to try to force the market to accept gas-guzzling, defect-prone vehicles that no longer had appeal to younger buyers.

By 2007, humility had triumphed. Toyota is one of the most successful corporations in the world. Its coffers are stuffed with cash, and its securities command a premium. As this is written, Toyota Motors has almost gained first-place honors in automobile sales in the United States.

On the other hand, once great and powerful General Motors and Ford are struggling for survival. Talk of potential bankruptcy surrounds them. Their bonds have been accorded non-investment-grade status. Never in our lifetime has the biblical injunction "Pride goes before destruction, a haughty spirit before a fall"[3] been more dramatically played out.

> *The Japanese humbled themselves to listen to the markets.... By 2007, humility had triumphed.*

In truth, few of us are free from pride. The temptations to pride are constantly bombarding us in motion pictures, television, radio, magazines, the Internet. People are being assessed throughout their lives: grades and awards in school, athletic achievement and championships, contests of strength and beauty. The assessment continues in life's work, employee evaluations, peer review, promotion, tenure, and the perks of power—the corner office, the company car, salary and bonus, club memberships, even office furniture.

Each step along the way is an invitation to pride.

Sometimes the symbols of rank become both petty and ludicrous. I once read the story of a company that moved its headquarters into a new office building. An assistant vice president of the company was assigned a new office that he felt was quite an improvement over his former quarters. One day after he had moved in, two workmen appeared at his door with a work order. Then they carefully measured the carpet in the office and proceeded to cut away a border three feet from each wall. When asked by the astounded executive what they were doing, they replied, "You don't rate wall-to-wall carpeting."

Imagine a corporate hierarchy so precise that executives were made to feel superior or inferior based on the borders of their office carpets. Imagine some executive sitting behind a closed door in a tiny office in some gigantic downtown skyscraper thinking to himself, *I am superior to others because I have wall-to-wall carpeting in my office*. Pride, you see, can come in many forms.

In today's world, money is the measuring stick of achievement and the source of sickening pride and ostentation.

A relatively recent phenomenon in the financial

world is the so-called hedge fund. Such funds are lightly regulated and cater primarily to large endowments and rich investors. Hedge funds are free to buy stocks or short stocks, buy options or complex derivatives. More recently, hedge funds (either singly or joined with others) have begun buying and selling entire businesses, some priced in the tens of billions of dollars. Because of their financial successes, many of these hedge funds have grown into financial behemoths with remarkable power. Along with success has come the incredible earning potential of the hedge fund principals. Hedge funds customarily charge a management fee of 2 percent of all the money they manage plus 20 percent of all profits. Recent disclosures revealed that the average income in 2006 of large hedge fund managers was a mind-numbing $350 million each.

Imagine a corporate hierarchy so precise that executives were made to feel superior or inferior based on the borders of their office carpets.

Pride cries out for an ostentatious display of such treasure. Obviously a person cannot walk around with his bank and brokerage statements pinned on his suit. So what to do? Begin an orgy of buying or building something so grand that the world will take notice.

In the April 13, 2007, edition of the *Wall Street Journal*, there appeared a story that Suzanne Saperstein, divorced wife of the founder of Metro Networks, was selling her Beverly Hills home, modeled after the palace of King Louis XIV at Versailles, for $125 million—the same price Donald Trump was asking for his Palm Beach, Florida, mansion. Three months later, the *New York Times* announced that Prince Bandar was putting up his Hala Ranch in Aspen, Colorado, for $135 million. These prices break the record set by financier Ronald Perelman in the sale of his Palm Beach home for $70 million. In the same issue of the *Journal* that announced the Saperstein sale, there were real estate listings for $59 million, $8.5 million, $20 million, and many at $3 to $5 million.

The race for status of possessions is not just limited to houses, art, and antiques.

Trophies of pride are not limited to palatial estates. Twenty years ago, I was shocked when Kerry Packer, Australian billionaire, bid $53 million for the painting *Irises* by impressionist Vincent van Gogh. But that was eclipsed in later years by the $76 million bid for Van Gogh's *Portrait of Dr. Gachet*. More recently, a self-portrait by Pablo Picasso was sold at auction for more than $100 million. Will there be an end to this madness?

The race for status of possessions is not just limited to houses, art, and antiques. Mega-yachts are the latest toys, with sizes up to four hundred feet in length and complete with helicopter pads and speedboat docks, selling at $250 million to $400 million.

No thinking person needs a $100 million home or yacht or painting. The message is clear: "Look at me. I am a success. I have a trophy wife. I own a trophy home, a trophy art collection, a trophy business, a trophy floating or flying palace. My trophies are grander than anybody's, so that makes me something special."

The *New York Times* recently ran a story titled "The Perils of Being Suddenly Rich." It concerned a San Francisco entrepreneur named David Hayden who started two Internet companies, Magellan and Critical Path. Although Magellan was not successful, in 1999 Robertson-Stephens, a premier investment banking house, took Critical Path public at $24 a share. With market action, the stock rose to a point where David Hayden had paper profits of up to $200 million.

Then Hayden lost touch with reality and developed a sense of hubris that he was impregnable to losses and defeats. A psychiatrist studying the cases of people like him coined the term *sudden wealth syndrome*, a fantasy that things can only go up.

Hayden sold $45 million worth of stock and borrowed tens of millions more against his remaining stock. He bought a 7,000-square-foot house in a wealthy neighborhood in San Francisco for $8 million, spending millions more gutting and renovating it. Then he bought a $4 million property in Sun Valley, Idaho. He put a down payment on a Gulfstream jet, invested in several start-up companies, drove a Ferrari, and even bought a half interest in an original copy of the Declaration of Independence.

Some of his coworkers were taken aback by his excesses. According to the *Times*, "I was embarrassed for him," said Wayne Correia, one of the original cofounders of Critical Path. "It was the worst case of nouveau riche you can possibly imagine."

Then Hayden's stock holdings in Critical Path crashed to $2 a share. He was left in debt to Robertson-Stephens for an adjudicated sum of $23,828,209.60 plus interest. There are liens on most of his assets, and the possibility of bankruptcy remains.

Again quoting the *Times*, "Hayden concedes . . . 'Dining with presidents is a heady thing. It can turn even the most well-grounded head.'" Humility would have brought on caution, simple living, fiscal restraint, and prudent hedging of his stock portfolio. Selfishness sent him on a wild and reckless spending spree. Pride said, "I am invincible, nothing can happen to me. I am important. I dine with presidents." Now Hayden is a ridiculed poster boy for an article with the subhead "Entrepreneurs who lost a fortune through poor money management."

Hayden lost touch with reality and developed a sense of hubris that he was impregnable to losses and defeats.

How far removed is the spirit of materialistic pride from the words of Jesus Christ, who said, "One's life does not consist in the abundance of the things he possesses,"[4] and "What is highly valued among men is detestable in God's sight"[5]?

Pride says, "I have made it. It's mine to enjoy. I will live large whenever and however I please."

Humility says, "I have nothing that was not given me by God. I am on this earth for a very short time and after that, eternity. When I die I can take nothing with me. Therefore, I am a life tenant of God's resources and will use them to please God and help others."

Regrettably, pride is not merely a private matter. Just as pride on the part of emperors, kings, and presidents can lead to war among nations, even so individual pride can lead inevitably to legal war, corporate war, bitter labor disputes, character assassination, theft, and even murder.

The apostle James summed it up this way: "What is

Pride is not merely a private matter.

causing the quarrels and fights among you? Don't they come from the evil desires at war within you? You want what you don't have, so you scheme and kill to get it. You

are jealous of what others have, but you can't get it, so you fight and wage war to take it away from them. . . . As the Scriptures say, 'God opposes the proud but favors the humble.'"[6]

I close this chapter with a mention of the man whose name is synonymous with materialistic excess, Donald Trump. No American in history has affixed his own name to as many highly visible trophies—Trump Tower, Trump Taj Mahal Casino, Trump Air, Trump Estates. Whatever he touches is filled with gaudy and ostentatious excess. He has given a whole new meaning to the term *nouveau riche*. He boasts of his economic success and the ratings success of his television show *The Apprentice*. He even sued a publication that said his net worth was only $200 million, not multiple billions. Yet remarkably Donald Trump has become the poster boy of the modern materialistic age—the condominiums bearing his name quickly sell out at stratospheric prices; his books on wealth creation are best sellers; and his television show is a ratings hit. America, perhaps the world, looks at him and sees its own dreams of pride, opulence, and success.

But when human life ends and eternity begins, who then is the winner and who is the loser? The wife of Sandy Weill, former head of the giant bank Citigroup, is reported to have put it well, paraphrasing the German proverb "There are no pockets in shrouds."

CHAPTER 3

"ONE WHO SERVES"

Plenty of people wish to become devout,
but no one wishes to be humble.

FRANÇOIS, DUC DE LA ROCHEFOUCAULD

If pride is the taproot of all sin and evil in the universe, then it would logically follow that the opposite of pride would be the greatest virtue. If most people with spiritual understanding were asked to name the greatest virtue, they would instinctively reply, "Love is the greatest virtue." The *Shema* of the Jews commands love of the one God, and almost every Christian Sunday school child can recite John 3:16, "For God so loved the world. . . . "

Yet I would submit that the countervailing virtue to the greatest source of evil is not love, but humility. Indeed the New Testament tells us that God's plan to redeem a fallen universe involved a supreme act of love, but the love was clothed with a humility that was in every detail a counterpart to the rebellion of Lucifer, the most powerful of all the angels.

Here is how the apostle Paul described it: "Though he [Jesus Christ] was God, he did not think of equality with God as something to cling to. Instead, he gave up his divine privileges; he took the humble position of a slave and was born as a human being. When he appeared in human form, he humbled himself in obedience to God and died a criminal's death on a cross. Therefore, God elevated him to the place of highest honor and gave him the name above all other names, that at the

The countervailing virtue to the greatest source of evil is not love, but humility.

name of Jesus every knee should bow, in heaven and on earth and under the earth."[1]

Lucifer said, "I will ascend to heaven; above the stars of God,"[2] through pride and rebellion. Jesus Christ determined in His heart, "I will surrender the trappings of power and will obey God even unto a criminal's death." Then God says, "Because You have humbled Yourself, I will raise You to the heights of heaven." Do you see the contrast?

Jesus Christ was born not in a palace, but in a stable. He rested not in a satin-lined bassinet but in a feed trough for cattle. His parents were not rich but were humble artisans. In His early days, Jesus was misunderstood and ridiculed, even called illegitimate and crazy. He humbly submitted to the wishes of His parents, humbly submitted to the rite of baptism in the Jordan River, and always lived in obedience to God. He never acquired property or other worldly possessions. He told His followers that He was among them as a servant, and that true greatness consisted in serving others. The night before His death, He demonstrated the message of humility when He stripped to a loincloth and performed the task of a slave, washing His disciples' dusty feet.

Satan lives out pride, arrogance, and rebellion. Jesus Christ lived out total humility, love, and sacrifice. The penalty of pride, arrogance, and rebellion is eternal separation from God. The reward of humility and obedience is eternal bliss in God's presence.

Shifting from the eternal to our everyday lives, what, we may inquire, are the benefits of humility? The benefits are many in every way. The author of the book of Proverbs put it quite well: "Humility and the fear of the LORD are riches and honor and life."[3]

Let's break this down. The first reward of humility gives us the fear of the Lord, which is the beginning of wisdom. Wisdom, in turn, is the sine qua non of all human achievement, be it commerce, politics, the arts, education, philanthropy, or social interaction. The humble person has access to God's wisdom and God's favor. "God," we are told, "resists the proud, but gives grace to the humble."[4]

The second reward of humility is wealth. I have known a number of very rich people. Most are quiet, reserved, and very intelligent. They made their money by listening, learning, and seeking ways to serve. But to the average person, wealth can mean a comfortable income and a secure retirement. Such a status is promised to the one who is humble.

The humble person has access to God's wisdom and God's favor.

The third reward of humility is honor. Honor comes in many sizes. It can be love and respect from a spouse and children. It can be affection from friends, neighbors, or colleagues. It can be a place on a winning team or an individual sales award. It can be a political victory or a good report card in school. Those who are humbled will be recognized and honored.

The fourth reward of humility is life. What is more desired above all than robust good health? No amount of money can compensate for wasting cancer, diabetes, Parkinson's disease, or Alzheimer's. A promising life cut short in its flower by an automobile crash or other unexpected accident is indeed tragic.

Humble people follow the rules; proud people feel the rules were made to be broken. A doctor friend of mine told me that at the Ohio hospital where he worked, youthful motorcyclists were referred to as "spare parts." Reckless youths feel that no accident will come to them, so they race motorcycles down crowded highways, or they drag race, BASE jump, or try ever-more-hazardous extreme sports, and many wind up maimed or dead ("spare parts" for those seeking healthy donor organs).

Humble people follow the wise advice of doctors, nutritionists, and physical therapists, and begin to achieve radiant health.

Humble people follow the wise advice of doctors, nutritionists, and physical therapists, and begin to achieve radiant health. Proud people ignore the rules and are self-indulgent with food, alcohol, tobacco, and narcotics. They find themselves faced with morbid obesity, adult-onset diabetes, coronary artery disease, various cancers, and a host of the maladies of early senility.

Think of the prize—wisdom, a comfortable living, favorable recognition, and robust health. Humility carries many other benefits, but these four indeed make the quest for humility worthwhile.

Many who consider humility reject it out of hand for one simple reason—they refuse to be someone's door-mat to be insulted, rejected, pushed around, and abused. They consider humility to be synonymous with weakness, and weakness is not for them.

These people have it all wrong. Some of the strongest and most effective people are also humble.

I am an avid horseman. Thirty years ago, I read of a remarkable breed of German horses who were the off-spring of the few survivors of the nightmare that was called the "Long Trek," when the battered German army struggled home from Hitler's ill-fated invasion of Russia. A German horse breeder had moved to my home state, imported several of these horses, and began breeding and selling them.

I drove up to the lady's farm, and before the day was out had purchased an elegant yearling Trakehner stal-lion—a descendant of the super-hardy trek survivors. His name was Aristocrat, but I called him Baby.

In three years, Aristocrat had grown into a magnifi-cent adult. He was 16.2 hands high, had powerful shoulders and hindquarters, and weighed at least twelve hundred pounds.

I sent him to school—first to a trainer who taught him remarkable obedience, then to a professional who schooled him to proficiency in what is called second-level dressage.

Aristocrat was beautiful and talented. He won the state championship at his level of dressage, then he picked up some ribbons in a three-day event where he was asked to gallop a four-and-a-half-mile obstacle course one day, perform stadium jumping the second day, and execute precision dressage the third.

He would bow if touched on his left leg. He would kneel if touched on both legs. If asked, he would perform flying changes of lead every fourth step. He would gallop at a touch and stop at a touch. He was controlled by pressure from my seat and legs and a light squeezing of my hands on the reins. At times, I would close my eyes, think in pictures, and he seemed to respond to what I was thinking.

Yet Aristocrat was a big, powerful stallion, perfectly capable of killing a rider one-sixth his size. I have seen him go after another stallion with nostrils flaring, teeth bared, squealing for battle.

To me, Aristocrat embodies biblical meekness and humility—enormous power and ability completely under control. Aristocrat had the power to kill, to perform great feats of athleticism, yet all that power was yielded to the control of a skilled rider.

Reaching back into antiquity, we learn that the great lawgiver Moses was the most humble man in all the earth. He was meek and humble, but never a doormat.

Some of the strongest and most effective people are also humble.

Moses is the biblical example of humility in ancient times. Moses was raised in the house of Pharaoh, the most powerful ruler of his day. According to legend, Moses was a skilled warrior who had been trained in all the wisdom of Egyptian science and statecraft. One day when he happened upon an Egyptian mistreating a Hebrew, he killed the Egyptian in hand-to-hand combat.

Fearing the consequences, Moses fled into the desert where he lived among the Midianites as a humble shepherd for forty years. Then Moses received a call from God to return to Egypt carrying only a shepherd's staff. His mission was to command Pharaoh to allow the six hundred thousand Hebrews living in Egypt to depart the country with all their possessions.

In the process, Moses fearlessly confronted Pharaoh, never diminished his demands, and, after ten devastating plagues, led the entire nation of Israel out of Egypt, through forty years in the Sinai, and finally to the border of the Promised Land. During those forty years, Moses dealt with multiple rebellions, spiritual apostasy, a seduction to immorality, a punishing environment, and warfare against opposing nations. Through it all, he brought his people a code of laws and regulations that still serve as a guide for Christians and Jews some thirty-five hundred years later.

With only one notable exception of disobedience, God's report about Moses was that he was "faithful in all My house."[5] But more particularly, this man filled with God's power, courage, and extraordinary wisdom was said to be "more humble than anyone else on the face of the earth."[6] If Moses is the model of biblical humility, then the appropriate description of humility must be great courage, strength, and ability totally under God's control.

Under no circumstances is the humble man weak, cowardly, or indecisive. Nor is he society's doormat. The same cannot be said of the proud man, whose pride can't see his own weakness.

RELATIVE STRENGTH

They that know God will be humble;
they that know themselves cannot be proud.

JOHN FLAVEL

When I reached the age of sixty, I began a serious study of exercise, nutrition, and health. I wanted to find out about the mechanisms that kept my body functioning and the hormones and chemicals that regulated those mechanisms.

I was astounded as I began to contemplate the exquisite relation between the elements of my life cycle code. For starters, I learned that the DNA code that makes up one human being is the equivalent of a library of one thousand volumes, each containing five hundred pages of single-spaced type of five-letter words.

I learned that there are five hundred thousand neural connections between one of my eyes and my brain, and that the brain is so complex that no computer has been built to equal it.

I haven't seen the equivalent in today's microcircuits, but in the days of the old vacuum-tube computers, it was estimated that a computer to equal the ability of the human brain would require a housing the size of the Empire State Building and water with the physical energy of Niagara Falls to cool it.

A fact equally wonderful in the preprogrammed life cycle is that little children are born with billions of extra brain cells. They can quickly learn languages, computer skills, music, and art. It is said that between the ages of four and five, a child can learn the equivalent of a four-year college education. This childish brain is somewhat undifferentiated, and yet at puberty the learning facility shifts somewhat to more purposeful activity to prepare for an adult life.

At this time, the glandular control mechanism releases a flood of human growth hormone. A growth spurt takes place, along with the appearance of male or female secondary sex characteristics. The human being is prepared for reproduction. At age twenty there begins a decline in the production of human growth hormone, testosterone, and DHEA so that by age fifty, these vital hormones are only minimally present. Women enter menopause, and the master regulator, the pineal gland, determines, "You can no longer reproduce, so it is time to shut you down." The slow, inexorable march toward senility and death follows.

As I contemplated this brilliantly planned cycle of life and death, and I considered the complexity of individual cells, the circulatory system, the function of serotonin, melatonin, and the interaction of chemicals that work to cause synapses in the human brain, I was frankly in awe. To think that God created this marvelous mechanism we call the body, and with it also meticulously programmed a seventy-year or one-hundred-and-twenty-year life cycle in each one of us with the appropriate hormonal cascades at each level of life. The Bible tells us that we are "fearfully and wonderfully made."[1] My response may seem ridiculous, but I blurted out, "God, You really are smart!"

There are five hundred thousand neural connections between one of my eyes and my brain.

If we can sense awe and wonder at the complexity of our own bodies, how much is this awe and wonder magnified in the presence of the cosmos? The psalmist wrote, "When I look at your heavens, the work of your fingers, the moon and the stars, which you have set in place, what is man that you are mindful of him, and the son of man that you care for him?"[2]

I am privileged as host of a daily television program to be able to interview an ongoing parade of fascinating people. On one occasion, I sat entranced as an Israeli astrophysicist with a doctorate from MIT outlined the latest thinking of the world's cosmologists. Through the years, there have been ten major theories of the origins of the cosmos. The current consensus centers on what is called the Big Bang. This theory posits that some fifteen billion years ago an incredibly dense clump of matter came into being with gravitational force beyond calculation, and then exploded with such power that matter, gas, and energy raced forth in all directions at the speed of light.

If we can sense awe and wonder at the complexity of our own bodies, how much is this awe and wonder magnified in the presence of the cosmos?

My astrophysicist guest then followed with even more startling observations. According to him, the informed consensus of his peers is that the universe is "tuned for life." In other words, there existed in the universe the necessary conditions for human life to flourish on earth. In order for that to happen, the material universe needed to be in such exquisite balance that the gravitational pull of all matter is not so strong that the universe will collapse on itself or so weak that it will expand out of existence.

With the huge distances involved in the universe, we would now be considering mass and energy beyond our calculation. But in the beginning, fifteen billion years ago, the amount of matter needed to provide universal equilibrium in the year 2000 would have required so fine a measurement that if the initial mass had varied up or down by a factor of 10 to the 26th power, there would have been no life on earth. Ten to the 26th power is less than a flyspeck.

Can I begin to contemplate the unfathomable wisdom of God? How can there be a being so wise and powerful that He could calculate to a flyspeck the precise amount of matter needed to bring forth life in His vast universe after an elapsed time of fifteen billion years?

I spend summer vacations on the top of a 4,100-foot mountain in western Virginia. On a clear evening, I can see brilliant stars and a band of what appears to be a gossamer cloud. This is the Milky Way—the name that we give to the galaxy of which our solar system is a part. Does not a mere human being shrink into insignificance in light of the magnificence of so great a Creator?

One of my favorite American heroes is a man born to slave parents near Diamond Grove, Missouri, in

1864. The Civil War was ending, and times were hard for blacks. George Washington Carver grew up poor and was denied an education because of his race. That didn't stop him from falling in love with the wonders of nature and the God who created them.

Does not a mere human being shrink into insignificance in light of the magnificence of so great a Creator?

Carver later went to high school and then even later attended college. At the age of thirty he earned a degree in agricultural science from Iowa State University. In 1896, he completed his master's degree and was asked to join the faculty of Tuskegee Institute, a trade school for blacks in Alabama.

There this deeply religious man began the work that revolutionized the agriculture of the South. He referred to God as "Mr. Creator." This is the dialogue that reportedly took place between them:

CARVER   Mr. Creator, show me the secrets of Your universe.

MR. CREATOR   Little man, your mind is too small to comprehend My universe. I will show you the secrets of the peanut.

CARVER	Mr. Creator, what do I do with the peanut?
MR. CREATOR	Take it apart.
CARVER	Then what?
MR. CREATOR	Put it back together again.

And so, George Washington Carver humbly obeyed God's command. He took apart the peanut. Then, as he put it back together, there came forth three hundred products like paint, plastics, cooking oil, and, of course, peanut butter. The Creator then showed him the sweet potato, and from that revelation came one hundred different products. The Creator showed him how to invent synthetics such as marble and plywood, and even the dye that is still used in Crayola crayons.

Carver's work not only revolutionized Southern agriculture, but it also revolutionized the food, paint, and plastics industries of the world. Carver could have been rich, but he chose to live humbly to help poor blacks in need of education.

Often he was heard to say, "The Lord has guided me," and "Without my Savior, I am nothing."

For each one of us, only when our eyes are opened like those of George Washington Carver to the majesty of the Creator and His wisdom that is beyond understanding can we place ourselves and our accomplishments in the proper prospective. Only then can we experience true humility. Only then can we have access to the "fear of the LORD [which] is the beginning of wisdom."[3]

Moses was raised to rank and privilege. It took an escape from a possible execution, plus forty years as a solitary shepherd on the back side of the wilderness to rid him of pride and prepare him to be a humble vessel in God's hands.

My personal background was not as exalted, nor was my life's work as extraordinary, but there have been instructive parallels. I, too, was raised to privilege. My father was a senior United States senator. In my background is one of the most distinguished families in Colonial Virginia from which came a signer of the Declaration of Independence and two United States presidents. A distant grandfather was a delegate from Orange County along with James Madison to the Virginia Assembly that ratified the United States Constitution. My ancestry is traced back to the crowned heads of Europe and is listed in the book *Living Descendants of Blood Royal (In America)*. I was given a superb education that included study at a top prep school, a top undergraduate university, and a Juris Doctor degree from Yale Law School. As a reward after college, I was permitted to take a survey course called The Arts in Britain Today at the University of London. Then I learned business in New York at a giant multinational corporation, W. R. Grace and Company.

Carver could have been rich, but he chose to live humbly to help poor blacks in need of education.

There was enough money from my parents and my earnings to afford a fraternity, drinking parties, nightclubs, gambling, and as much of a dissolute life as I could handle. My goal was to be successful in business and make a lot of money.

But like Moses, something happened to me. I became desperately unhappy. The life of seeking money and pleasure that I was living was empty. After a profound inner struggle, I determined to serve God. In the process I met Jesus Christ, and He radically altered my life—my desires, my motives, and my purposes.

This experience led me to leave the business world and begin a three-year master's degree course at the New York Theological Seminary. There I studied the Bible; but more important, I learned to fast and pray, hear God's voice, and submit to His will. Moses spent forty years freeing himself from his privileged position in Egypt. I spent three years doing much the same.

After a profound inner struggle, I determined to serve God.

After seminary, I spent a month in concentrated prayer. God's word to me was to sell my possessions, give the money to the poor, and get ready to follow Him. I moved my wife and three little red-headed, blue-eyed children into Brooklyn's declining Bedford-Stuyvesant neighborhood to live in an old brownstone parsonage that could best be described as an inter-racial commune. Looking back, I can laughingly say, "I was into communes before communes were cool!" Here was what was once a hotshot young business executive and his family now living in a house along with an assortment of unusual people, including a for-mer madam and a slow-witted giant from the Caribbean Islands. We subsisted on vegetables that we scrounged from the leftovers at the Fulton Street Market, bread from the day-old bread store, and what-ever our hands came upon.

Then I left Brooklyn with my family, an old DeSoto automobile, and seventy dollars to buy a run-down UHF television station in Portsmouth, Virginia. After I got there, a friend sent me thirty-five dollars, which I used to obtain a corporate charter for a new nonprofit corporation titled The Christian Broadcasting Network, Inc. The charter was granted on January 11, 1960. A few days later, I received our first contribution—three rumpled one-dollar bills. Two weeks later, this Yale Law School graduate timidly approached the Bank of Virginia to open a corporate bank account with the grand total of three dollars.

The path to humility is not easy. We had little or no money for food. I knew that soybeans were a near-perfect food, and I was able to buy a seventy-pound sack of soybeans for two dollars. Soybeans for us were like the manna of the ancient Hebrews. We had soybean waffles, soybean pancakes, and split-soybean soup. My children hated soybeans, but I explained to them that this was God's provision to keep us alive. As a child, I was used to rib roasts, porterhouse steaks, country ham, fried chicken—an abundance of everything. In my new state, I considered it a great treat to find a special on a cheap grade of bologna at twenty-nine cents a pound to eat with stale bread.

I was learning to be content with what I had. I was learning not to complain, but to give thanks in everything. I was learning to trust the Lord instead of my own abilities. I was learning not to despise the day of small beginnings. Without my realizing what was happening, I was being trained by the Lord to develop the spiritual muscles needed to sustain what was to become one of the largest and most effective broadcast ministries on earth. And I was being taught that without Him, I could do nothing; but with His wisdom and power, nothing was impossible.

As the great Presbyterian Bible teacher Dr. Donald Grey Barnhouse once remarked, "God uses oak trees, not mushrooms. The graces of God and the ministries He assigns each of us are only formed through time, trials, and testings. Oak trees grow slowly, but they are here to last. Mushrooms pop up overnight, but they lack both strength and permanence."

In its first year of operation, the Christian Broadcasting Network (CBN) had a total income of $8,000; the second year, $20,000.

Fast-forward forty-seven years, and CBN is now broadcasting into 200 countries in as many as 60 languages to an estimated worldwide audience of 300,000,000. We have 70 international counseling centers, 17 production centers worldwide, and 33 different language Internet Web sites. CBN produces more

Christian Arabic-language television programs than any other organization in the world. Our headquarters in Kiev in the Ukraine has received 14,000,000 letters from all over the former Soviet Union. It sustains 70,000 cell churches all over what is now known as the Commonwealth of Independent States (or C.I.S.). In 2006, an estimated 40,000,000 people made professions of faith in Jesus Christ because of one of the hundreds of programs CBN produces.

> *I was being taught that without Him, I could do nothing; but with His wisdom and power, nothing was impossible.*

The sister organization founded in 1978, Operation Blessing Relief and Development, distributes more than one hundred million pounds of food and supplies to the needy in the United States each year, and supports orphanages, homes for the elderly, medical missions, well digging, and disaster relief worldwide. It is estimated that Operation Blessing has given out some $1.1 billion in medicine and relief supplies since its inception.

Regent University, also founded in 1978, has become the preeminent evangelical graduate university in the United States with master's and doctoral degrees in law, government, communications, leadership, business, divinity, education, and psychology. The Regent

Law School teams in Moot Court and Negotiating took the national first-place honors that, in the American Bar Association contests, had once been held by Yale Law School and Harvard Law School.

Along the way, we created the Family Channel, which became one of the ten largest cable networks in the United States with some seventy-eight million paid subscribers. We then took it public as International Family Entertainment, Inc., and ultimately sold it for $1.8 billion.

In its first year of operation, the Christian Broadcasting Network (CBN) had a total income of $8,000; the second year, $20,000.

As all these things happened, I was more like a bystander to what God was doing. He would tell me what to do to get things going, and then I had the delight of participating with Him in a constant flow of miraculous blessing. I constantly had to numb myself to any sense of pride, because I realized that I was merely part of a plan laid out by an all-wise God before the world began.

Over the years, I have been able to articulate a clear philosophy. I give credit to the Lord for all the successes, and I take the blame for all the mistakes. I would be lying to say that I don't appreciate the successes and triumphs, but I appreciate them as God's successes, not mine. My goal is to emulate the sentiment of the apostle Paul, who wrote, "God forbid that I should boast except in the cross of our Lord Jesus Christ, by whom the world has been crucified to me, and I to the world."[4]

CHAPTER 5

A MESSENGER OF SATAN

*We must view humility as one of the most essential
things that characterizes true Christianity.*

JONATHAN EDWARDS

The apostle Paul wrote in his second letter to the
Corinthian church of a spiritual experience in which
he was "caught up to the third heaven,"[1] where he saw
sights and heard sounds that a mortal should not experience. An encounter like this could have filled him
with overwhelming pride and shattered all vestiges of
humility, which, in turn, would have completely
destroyed his walk with God and the effectiveness of
his ministry. But God had the perfect antidote to the
poison. Paul put it this way: "Lest I should be exalted
above measure by the abundance of the revelations, a
thorn in the flesh was given to me, a messenger of
Satan to buffet me, lest I be exalted above measure."[2]

Exactly what this messenger of Satan was is not
known. Some speculate that Paul had a chronic dis-
charging eye infection. Others, without justification,
suggest epilepsy. The best explanation would be the
constant harassment Paul received wherever he went

from his fellow Jews and later the Romans. He was stoned, beaten repeatedly, lied about, harassed, hauled into court, and imprisoned. He despaired of life. He certainly never had time to feel exalted. In fact, Paul described himself as the "offscouring"[3] of the earth, like one of the men slated to die who marched last in the triumphal procession of a Roman general.

Paul described himself as the "offscouring" of the earth.

And, as an aside, we learn that in order to ensure humility during the triumphal procession of a Roman battle hero, there was stationed in his chariot a slave whose task was simply to whisper over and over, "You, too, shall die."

Paul was given his "messenger of Satan"[4] to ensure humility, and I am persuaded that to those God loves, when they achieve spiritual or material success, lest they be "exalted above measure,"[5] there will invariably be a modern-day equivalent. It can be a harassing in-law, a despotic employer, a vicious competitor, a series of lawsuits, or sporadic health issues. The possibilities are endless.

For almost fifty years, my "messenger of Satan" has been our local newspaper, which, through a succession of publishers, editors, and reporters, has seldom failed to attack, slander, belittle, or misrepresent the work I do. Since I, as a Christian, am instructed to turn the other cheek when someone strikes me, over the years I can say in jest that my head has been spinning like a top, turning one cheek and then the other before their attacks.

With few notable exceptions, the press in the United States and Europe display virulent hostility toward conservative evangelical Christianity. With the advent of political correctness, most groups in our society, except evangelical Christians, are protected from verbal abuse. Evangelical Christians are fair game for ongoing slander and ridicule. A few years ago during the confirmation hearings of a nominee to the Supreme Court (United States circuit court judge Clarence Thomas), I urged my television audience to call their United States senators at the U.S. Capitol in support of Thomas. The response was so overwhelming that not only was the Capitol switchboard overloaded, but all the circuits into Washington, D.C., began to shut down.

The *Washington Post* assigned a reporter to investigate. His story on the front page above the fold was that the calls came from the "followers" of Pat

Robertson who were "poor, uneducated, and easy to command." This resulted in a flood of angry letters to the *Post* from people "richer and better educated" than the *Post* reporter, who brought forth this rejoinder, "But *everyone knows* that my assessment was correct" (emphasis added).

With few notable exceptions, the press in the United States and Europe display virulent hostility toward conservative evangelical Christianity.

The "everyone knows" comment indicates that the perceived judgment of the media elite is that only poor, uneducated yahoos can possibly believe in God, regard the Holy Bible as an inspired book to serve as a guide for life, and live out truly Christian lives of marital fidelity, honesty, and patriotic service.

More recently, this hostility has taken on a sinister tone. Wealthy Hollywood mogul Norman Lear founded a left-wing lobbying group called People for the American Way. Their total thrust was to blunt the pro-family agenda of evangelical Christians. A sister organization, called Americans United for Separation of Church and State, was organized by an operative from the left-leaning, antireligious American Civil Liberties

Union. More recently, Hungarian-born billionaire George Soros helped finance an organization called Media Matters.

People for the American Way, Americans United, and Media Matters have assigned paid staffers to record the audio and video of every word I utter on television. If they can find anything slightly controversial, they take it out of context, add or subtract words or phrases from my speech, then insert their own editorial explanation that alters what was said. This material is then sent to an individual at the Associated Press office in Washington who, in turn, feeds the doctored statement around the world to my discredit and embarrassment.

One or all of the three left-wing activist groups altered my words to make it appear that I had said God struck down Sharon.

A case in point. When Prime Minister Ariel Sharon was felled by a stroke, I said on television that Sharon was a good friend, that we had prayed together, and that I was hoping for his recovery. Then I said that the prophet Joel warns against those who "divided up my land."[6] I concluded, "Woe to any American president or quartet of nations or prime minister of Israel who divides God's land." Never, however, did I say that God struck Sharon for giving up Gaza.

However, one or all of the three left-wing activist groups altered my words to make it appear that I had said God struck down Sharon. The Associated Press carried the doctored statement worldwide. Then I was condemned by my Israeli friends and by my evangelical friends, and I was ridiculed throughout America.

To quell the storm, I was forced to make a humble public apology to Sharon's son and to the Israeli people on international television—for something I did not say!

But how could I be angry at the press or these three avowed enemies? They humiliate me, they bring me heartache, and they try to rob me of joy. They crowd me closer to God. But more particularly, they serve to ensure that I am brought low in humility to the very place where almighty God stands ready to bless me. How could I be angry at someone who ensures that I will receive from the Lord wisdom, riches, honor, and life?!

In my case, the agents of humility, the messengers of Satan who buffet, are not limited to the liberal media or left-wing advocacy groups. My staff estimates we receive eight or nine death threats each month. A bomb that was sent to me exploded in our mail room. Several years ago, a demented viewer who thought that because of the insight of my biblical teachings I was "reading his mind," entered the office of a North Carolina television station that aired our program, shot and killed the sales manager, then took the receptionist hostage. This tragedy brought a sobering realization of how fragile life is.

All of us face suffering, disease, family tragedies, and the death of loved ones. We have business reversals, missed opportunities, and see our hopes dashed. In short, we are human beings, and like it or not we humans live in a world where we are regularly confronted with death and sorrow. Moses wrote in Psalm 90, "Teach us to realize the brevity of life, so that we may grow in wisdom."[7] Only a proud fool feels that his money or his success could shield him from the pains of human existence. The wise humbly realize that their short life on earth will often be touched by sorrow, and then like a vapor they soon will fly away.

Like it or not we humans live in a world where we are regularly confronted with death and sorrow.

Within the biblical book of Genesis is a story of the grandson of the patriarch Abraham whose name was Jacob. At birth, Jacob grabbed the heel of his fraternal twin, Esau, in an attempt to prevent him from being born first. Jacob was presented as the crafty heel snatcher who tricked his older brother Esau out of both his birthright and his patriarchal blessing. Jacob was tricked by his uncle, Laban, in his choice of a wife, but Jacob returned the favor and tricked Laban out of the lion's share of his flocks.

In Jacob's favor was his spiritual nature. Despite his craftiness, it would seem that Jacob was governed by spirit and intellect, while Esau was governed by the demands of his body. The birthright entitled its holder to be the spiritual head of the family. Jacob wanted it, but Esau sold it for a bowl of lentil stew. The blessing was the key to material wealth, and Jacob provided an elaborate ruse with animal skins and hunting clothes to make his blind father, Isaac, believe that he, Jacob, was his hairy, firstborn son, Esau, the hunter.

After decades had elapsed, Jacob went back home to face Esau. After all those years, he was still relying on craft and artifice. He was scared of what might happen but was still proud enough to rely on his own skill to save him from Esau's anger.

The night before the encounter of the two brothers was to take place, a mighty angel appeared to Jacob. They began to wrestle. They wrestled all night. As dawn was breaking, the angel said, "Let me go." But

Jacob replied, "I will not let you go until you bless me."

Then the angel replied, "You have wrestled with God and with men, and have overcome. From now on you will no longer be known as Jacob (the trickster), but Israel, the prince with God." Then the angel touched Jacob's hip and crippled it. Jacob left the encounter hobbling on his staff.

Despite his craftiness, it would seem that Jacob was governed by spirit and intellect.

What lesson does this story have for us? In my opinion, the wrestling match was between an angel who represented the proud man (who had beaten his brother twice, fooled his father, and plundered his uncle), and the humble man (who valued the family's spiritual heritage and who now wanted God's blessing above all else). As dawn was breaking, the humble man won. The old Jacob was no more, but God's servant, Israel, came forth. However, to ensure that the proud old man did not return, the new man was physically crippled for life, totally dependent on God. He was then humble enough to be the progenitor of the sons who brought forth the twelve tribes that formed a great nation that, to this day, bears his new name, Israel.

BORN BETTER THAN YOU

We may as well try to see without eyes, or live without breath,
as to live in the spirit of religion without humility.

WILLIAM LAW

In the 1990s, I traveled to New Delhi in India to negotiate a contract to place some of our television programs on the Indian national television network, Doordarshan.

I was privileged to have dinner one evening at my hotel in Delhi with a bishop of the Pentecostal Church of India. This intelligent and godly man had a skin color that was gray black. I learned that because of his skin color, he was classified as an untouchable (they now are called Dalits).

He was quite open to discussing it, so I inquired at length about the practice in India that resulted in three hundred million Indian people being assigned an inferior status as untouchables. Here in summary is what I learned.

During the second century BC, the Indian subcontinent was supposedly invaded by northern tribes known as Aryans. The dark-skinned native Indians were subjugated by the fair-skinned Aryans, who proceeded to create in their Hindu religion a spiritual justification for their racial dominance. (This Aryan invasion is a matter of considerable controversy.)

The fair-skinned Brahmins were said to have come forth from the head of their supreme deity, Brahma.

Their highest order of society, the fair-skinned Brahmins, were said to have come forth from the head of their supreme deity, Brahma. Then each shade of skin color was said to originate from the lower parts of Brahma's body. The dark-skinned people were said to have come forth from under the feet of Brahma.

This racial injustice was coupled with a belief in karma, which held that a person's destiny is forever linked to his spirit and would be brought forth in never-ending cycles of material existence, a process that is called reincarnation.

So the karma of the dark-skinned people was to be perpetual mistreatment at the hands of the fair-skinned people. Until recent legislation was passed in India, the daily life of the untouchables was pure torment and misery.

The Brahmins believed that they would be defiled if even the shadow of an untouchable came upon them. Untouchable women could not use village wells lest their presence pollute those of a higher caste. Only the most menial jobs were open to untouchables, such as cleaning latrines, removing garbage, and sweeping the streets. In former years, they could be beaten unmercifully by upper-caste Indians for even the most minor real or imagined offense.

This entire wicked system was built on pride glossed over by a veneer of religiosity. "I belong to a higher caste, therefore I am superior to those beneath me." From this mind-set flows what comes next, "These inferior people are not worthy of the respect due my caste, so I am free to abuse them."

There seems to be something innate in human beings, something that wishes to assert superiority for its race, its clan, its ethnic group over all others. Just think, the Jews are the *chosen race*, and everyone else is a *goy*, which can be translated as "gentile" or "heathen." The Muslims think they are the *true believers*, and everyone else is an *infidel*. The Wahhabi sect believes that within Islam they are the *true believers*, and all other Muslims are *polytheists*. In Iraq, a bitter civil war is raging with countless deaths over whether

Ali, Mohammad's cousin, was the true heir to the Islamic tradition as the Shiites believe, or whether true Islam rests with the Sunnis and their descent from Mohammad.

There seems to be something innate in human beings, something that wishes to assert superiority for its race, its clan, its ethnic group over all others.

In pre–World World I Turkey, a hideous genocide was waged by the Muslim Turks against the Christian Armenians. In our day, the Serbian dictator Milosevic determined to cleanse his land of its Muslim inhabitants. More recently in Sudan, the Arab Muslim leaders are committing an ongoing brutal genocide against the black African Muslim population in a desert region of Sudan known as Darfur.

On my first visit to South Africa, before the most recent dramatic political transformation of that nation took place, I learned directly from President P. W. Botha the rationale for their apartheid system and his solution to a transition away from it. Advocates of apartheid believed that the races would be happier if they existed apart from one another. So there were rules and privileges for white people; rules, privileges, and restrictions for Indians and mulattoes (known as coloreds); and rules, privileges, and restrictions for black people. During my extensive visit, I discovered that the lot of the coloreds and blacks in South Africa was not nearly as onerous as has been portrayed in the popular media. Nevertheless, the white minority felt that they were superior to the black majority and, consequently, kept for themselves political power, police power, and the best share of the nation's wealth. As a consequence of racial pride, South Africa became a pariah nation among the community of nations. The stigma has only been cleansed by the dismantling of the hated apartheid system.

The pages of the world's history are filled with the clashes of tribes, clans, and religious adherents, each of whom presumed itself to be superior to the other. Perhaps the most insidious is the virulent hatred of the Jews by their blood cousins, the Arabs. Mohammad, after being rejected by the Jews of Medina as a great prophet, slaughtered the men of Medina, took their women, and then wrote in the Koran that the Jews were the descendants of apes and pigs. To this day, such incendiary teaching is being drilled into the minds of little children studying in Wahhabi madrassas both in Saudi Arabia and everywhere else where the Wahhabi version of Islam has spread. Even in Shiite-dominated Iran, President Mahmoud Ahmadinejad has called for the annihilation, presumably by nuclear weapons, of the entire nation of Israel.

We don't have to travel beyond our shores to experience the pride of race and its distasteful consequences. I grew up in the South at a time when black people were routinely referred to by the offensive term *niggers*, schools were segregated, buses were segregated, restrooms were segregated, lunchrooms were segregated, housing was segregated, voting was restricted, and business and employment opportunities for black people were severely limited. Humility says loud and clear, "All human beings are made in God's image. The color of my skin, the shape of my eyes, and the texture of my hair never make me superior to any other human being." America fought a war to end slavery, but it is taking a titanic political struggle to clear away the crippling disease of racial discrimination.

In the United States, pride fairly oozes from the pores of those who comprise the liberal elite in New York and Los Angeles. They fly over the great heartland of America, but they seldom humble themselves to realize that there is not only genuine American political thought, but great art, great literature, and great scholarship in a host of cities like Des Moines, Indianapolis, Milwaukee, Denver, Phoenix, and Houston.

I was born in a university town in Virginia, and from my earliest days I was taught that Virginia was the epicenter of culture and noble tradition. I met and married a lovely girl from Columbus, Ohio. When I first traveled to her home in the Columbus suburb of Bexley, we took a leisurely stroll down a nearby boulevard called Broad Street. We passed by a procession of stately, classically designed mansions. The Virginian in me blurted out, "I didn't know that there were houses like this in Ohio!" My wife, who has never let me forget that piece of arrogance, laughingly replied, "What did you think we lived in out here, cabins and tepees?" In truth, my reality sixty years ago, until that moment, was of James River plantations, Mt. Vernon, Monticello, Thomas Jefferson, and Robert E. Lee in Virginia, and steel mills, automobile factories, Abraham Lincoln, log cabins, and the "Little House on the Prairie" in the Midwest.

The pages of the world's history are filled with the clashes of tribes, clans, and religious adherents, each of whom presumed itself to be superior to the other.

The moral of that story is that ignorance feeds pride, and knowledge brings humility. Just realize the arrogance we displayed toward the Japanese. We fought them, we conquered them, and we occupied them. Their economy was in ruins. For a short time, I was part of the occupying force that had taken over their best hotels and their best golf courses and resorts, and that was in charge of rebuilding their entire economy.

We liked the Japanese as people, but their postwar economy was a joke. They did not have gasoline engines in their automobiles. Instead, there were taxis powered by charcoal burners located behind the backseats. It was always touch and go as to whether those things could climb to the top of even a modest hill. As I remember, smaller Japanese cities like Kyoto in 1951 lacked sewage, potable water, and a functioning electrical power grid. In short, we Americans were the superior experts in the midst of a semifeudal society that we looked down on.

There is not only genuine American political thought, but great art, great literature, and great scholarship in a host of cities.

In 1951, Korea was much more primitive. Many of the city streets were not paved, but were dusty, dirty trails. There was a virtual absence of those amenities we regard as normal in an advanced society. U.S. servicemen called the Koreans—at least the North Koreans—*gooks*, a term of scorn and disdain.

We were people fighting for freedom, and that is noble, but we reeked of pride and arrogance. Over sixty years later, that charge is still leveled against us around the world. And those "gooks" have become brilliant scientists and engineers, astute businessmen who are flooding our country with high-quality automobiles, advanced electronics, and consumer appliances. They have taken the lead in video games. The bigger Korean companies are building huge oil refineries and supertankers. North Korea possesses an estimated seven or eight nuclear bombs, plus the Taepo-Dong 1 and 2 missiles, the latter capable of reaching the United States. The formerly humble of the earth have seemingly risen to bring down the proud.

CHAPTER 7

LIKE A LITTLE CHILD

*By meditating upon Christ's humility, we shall
see how far we are from being humble.*

SAINT TERESA OF AVILA

The roads of ancient Judea were rocky and dusty. Those who walked these roads were soon tired and footsore. Jesus Christ was an itinerant preacher who walked in the hot sun with a group of disciples from small town to small town.

Although His body must have ached from physical exertion and privation, Jesus' focus was on His mission—and the grim knowledge that when they reached Jerusalem, He would be taken prisoner, falsely accused, and executed.

Yet, like their twenty-first-century counterparts, Jesus' disciples—the very people on whom would be built a religion that in our day would win to faith over 2.2 billion believers—were focused not on their leader's mission, but on their place and prestige. In their pride and self-interest, they seemed oblivious to Jesus' impending suffering and death. They actually began to argue among themselves who was the greatest. Remember, these were not crowned heads of state, nor were they captains of industry. No, this argument arose among twelve unlettered men with few possessions, walking along a dusty, rocky road in Judea. You see, pride and the absence of humility is not limited to the rich and powerful. It is a disease that can overcome us all if we are not vigilant.

You see, pride and the absence of humility is not limited to the rich and powerful.

Jesus quickly brought them to their senses. Your model, He explained to them, has been the system used by the Gentiles where the so-called great men lord it over other men, and dictators are called benefactors. But with you (He patiently explained), it must be different. You are all brothers. There is no rank or privilege separating you. Your measure of greatness is simply determined by your level of service to others. The great among you will be the servants, and the greatest will be the bondslave of all.

This principle is wildly counterintuitive to the prevailing thought of every age. Isn't the dream of a materialistic society to accumulate enough wealth to be set apart from others, to live on a country estate or in a gated community, to join an exclusive club or travel first-class? Isn't the dream to rise to be the boss—

captain of the team, labor leader, foreman, corporate vice president or president, headmaster, governor, chairman? To achieve some position so you can tell others what to do and be addressed with respect and deference?

But is the selfish materialistic dream the way to greatness? I don't think so. Greatness comes only from service. Think of those we consider great. Thomas Edison is a great man because he served every human being on earth with the gift of electric light. In the process, Edison acquired wealth. Wealth did not make him great. His service made him great. The wealth was a minor by-product.

In every culture today, handheld cell phones with text have become ubiquitous. At the touch of a keypad, satellite messages circle the globe with amazing clarity. Soon there will be a complete merging of telephone, television, computers, and the Internet. The world has come closer together as the pace of technological advancement reaches a feverish pitch. None of this would have been possible without the genius of Alexander Graham Bell, the inventor of the telephone—a great man who served the world of his day and countless millions more in future decades and centuries long after his death.

It is easy to think of those whose passion was to serve yet who gained material success. Henry Ford perfected the mass production of automobiles. Andrew Carnegie perfected the processing of steel. Bill Gates perfected the computer software needed to operate tens of millions of small computers. Sam Walton perfected a retail technique to lower the living costs of tens of millions of people. And Martin Luther King Jr. served the cause of freedom for millions of black Americans.

The level of greatness is measured by the extent of service. History will bear witness to the silent army of those who have served the cause of freedom, the cause of industrial progress, the arts, and especially the spiritual life of people. "For even the Son of Man came not to be served but to serve, and to give his life as a ransom for many."[1] Jesus had no wealth, no possessions, no army or navy, no earthly kingdom. Yet of all the people who have ever lived, He is considered the greatest—the bondslave of all.

Jesus' disciples needed more than one lesson to overcome their natural tendencies. He took a little child and set him upon His lap with these words, "I tell you the truth, unless you change and become like little children, you will never enter the kingdom of heaven."[2]

Not only were His followers to be servants, they also were to become like children. What characteristics of children should we seek to emulate? What is it about a child that becomes our model of humility?

First, a child is a model of humility because he is happy. Life is a great adventure filled with ever-expanding opportunities for fun.

I read recently that researchers had determined the health benefits of laughter. According to this report, an average child laughs

Greatness comes only from service.

four hundred times a day. I have four children and fourteen grandchildren. As a parent, I can remember back to the squeals of laughter that the silliest story or adult antic could provoke in a child. I can remember the reaction of my two-year-old daughter at the news of a proposed party or picnic. She would clap her hands and jump up and down in delight with cries of "Yippee, yippee, yippee!"

Pride fills us with self-conscious pseudosophistication. The proud man can't jump up and down or shout for joy. The humble man doesn't worry about the image, but rejoices in God's wonderful world. I remember being invited to sit with Clint Murchison in his owner's box at the Texas Stadium for a game between the Dallas Cowboys and the old Houston Oilers. It was a delightful experience. The greatest compliment paid me that day was by a young Christian businessman sitting behind me in the box: "I thought that you would be stiff and reserved, but you had so much fun you were like a little kid."

Life is a great adventure filled with ever-expanding opportunities for fun.

Second, a normal child is a model of humility because he is boundlessly curious: Why is grass green; why is the sky blue; why is the ocean salty; why is it cold in the winter; and, more recently, how do you build a computer? Unless we drill it out of them by the numbing experience of teaching to a standardized test, children will continue to explore new horizons with an open mind. That is humility.

Pride, on the other hand, thinks it knows all the answers, is too self-conscious to reveal lack of knowledge, and is sure there is no one able to enhance what it knows. I am amused when I think of a particularly brilliant Yale Law School classmate who was drafted into the army after graduation, then assigned the task of teaching mid-level officers complex intelligence theory. Here was a lowly private first class, teaching a class of arrogant captains, majors, and lieutenant colonels. To get his arrogant pupils in the proper frame of mind, I was told my classmate began his lecture with these words: "There are a number of people who know more about this subject than I do, but none of them happen to be in this room."

The humble are childlike because they never stop learning, they never stop seeking ways to improve, and they never stop asking questions. I remember once receiving a briefing from a research specialist that we had hired for a project. As he got deeper into arcane statistical theory, my eyes

Pride, on the other hand, thinks it knows all the answers.

started to glaze over. Since I was the CEO, and supposedly a knowledgeable professional, I was reluctant to state flat out that I did not have the vaguest idea what he was talking about. My pride would have required me to act as if this was material with which I was familiar, nod my head, smile, and thank him for his hard work.

On the other hand, in order to get my money's worth, I had to come clean. So I stopped his presentation and said candidly, "I don't understand what you are talking about. Would you please explain?"

At that, he looked a bit startled and said, "Your statement certainly is refreshing." Then he gave a simple explanation that was easy to understand and, as I recall, quite helpful. Humility won out and gained a benefit. Believe me, the urging of pride to save face and fake understanding had been very strong.

> *I was reluctant to state flat out that I did not have the vaguest idea what he was talking about.*

Another characteristic of a humble childlike spirit is complete dependence on someone more powerful. I recently read the story of Lois Wilson, the founder of Al-Anon, the family support group equivalent of Alcoholics Anonymous, which her husband had founded. Lois struggled during the pathetic battle that her charming and talented husband, Bill Wilson, waged to overcome the curse of alcoholism. Out of their struggle came the famous Twelve Step Plan to gain freedom from addiction. The foundation of the Twelve Steps was belief in a higher power. Bill Wilson's victory came when he not only surrendered to God, but enlisted the aid of another recovered alcoholic who knew what he was going through and was there to help him.

The entire concept of AA has been a humble acknowledgment of the problem, "I am an alcoholic," and a request for help. As long as an alcoholic proudly refuses to acknowledge that he or she has a problem, there will never be a true release from the addiction.

A little child has to rely on his parents for food, clothing, shelter, transportation, education—everything. In a normal home, a child must learn to trust the benevolence of the parent, to rely on the parents' wisdom, and to submit to the parents' authority.

There is a Sunday school song called "Trust and Obey." The writer of Proverbs put it even better: "Trust in the LORD with all your heart; do not depend on your own understanding. Seek his will in all you do, and he will show you which path to take."[3]

Only a person who has childlike humility will trust the Lord with all his heart without trying to second-guess the Lord or attempting to substitute human reason for divine wisdom. That type of trust can be nerve-racking, but the promised reward eclipses all fear: "He will show you which path to take."[4]

I would like to insert here a strong caveat to beware of false humility. In the early days of Christianity, there were the so-called pillar saints who spent months, or even years, in solitary self-deprivation trying to reach a sanctified existence. In truth, after a period of time many did not find holiness and humility. Instead, many of them became subject to wild fantasies and rampant pride. There is in common parlance the term *holier than thou*, which describes those who, because of their religious practices, consider themselves more holy than their friends and associates. This attitude is not holiness; it is sinful pride.

If a sprinter can run a 100-meter race in world-class time, he or she should not deny the fact with a self-deprecating "I feel like an old slowpoke."

All of us should rejoice in our gifts and talents whether our muscles are suitable for athletic accomplishment, whether we have a facility with words, whether we can perceive light and color in a gifted way, whether we have talent with numbers, selling, teaching, strategic planning, music, or dance, or whether our face and physique are admired.

True humility does not think of itself more highly than it should, nor does it boast. At the same time, true humility does not deny gifts and talents, but acknowledges them as gifts of God. True humility recognizes that there is nothing we have received that did not have its source outside ourselves. Humility says, "I have received a talent from the Lord. I will not deny it, but will use it for His glory."

CHAPTER 8

ONE FLESH

*Pure Christian humility disposes a person to take notice of
every thing that is good in others, and to make the
best of it, and to diminish their failings.*

JONATHAN EDWARDS

The most profound relationship that men and women
enter into during their lifetime is marriage. The book
of Genesis declares that marriage was instituted by
God, who pronounced, "Therefore a man shall leave
his father and mother and be joined to his wife, and
they shall become one flesh."[1] For the Christian, the
New Testament sanctified the marriage union even
further by comparing it to the mystical spiritual union
of Christ and His church.

The union between a man and his wife is to be complete—a coupling of two bodies, two minds, and two
spirits. Obviously, the sexual physical union is important, for by it human beings are given the power to
bring forth young lives made in the very image of
God. But marriage is not truly complete until a couple
is able to unite their lives in the rich tapestry of intel-
lectual and spiritual experience, hopes, and dreams.

In short, couples should not wall off any facet of their lives from one another. It becomes a tragedy when one partner in a marriage feels that he or she is intellectually or spiritually superior to the marriage partner. In such a marriage, the union does not extend beyond the physical. Consequently, the marriage is pitifully stunted.

Couples should not wall off any facet of their lives from one another.

A law school classmate of mine related the story of his college philosophy professor, a brilliant scholar of German ancestry. In the days of long-distance railroad travel, the professor always arranged for a Pullman sleeping berth for himself because he needed rest to ensure that his mind was clear for complex reasoning. We find no fault with his premise until we learn that he forced his wife and daughters to sit up all night in the coach section of the same train because, according to him, they were women and would never be called upon to bring forth the type of reasoned thought requiring a restful night's sleep.

Fortunately, the masculine arrogance typified by the German professor is seldom seen in a more enlightened Western world. Regrettably, this virulent poison pervades the Muslim Middle East. I am chairman of the humanitarian charity known as Operation Blessing International Relief and Development, Inc. Following the war in Afghanistan, Operation Blessing established feeding stations and medical clinics for the poor Afghan people. At one clinic, the head of our Afghan program, Kumar Periasamy, noticed a young woman receiving medical treatment and called her by her first name. At this greeting, the woman began to cry. When asked why she was crying, she revealed that during some eighteen years of marriage, not once had her husband addressed her by her name. To him she was little better than a cow or a donkey, in no way the equal of a male.

Humility declares that wives and husbands are to be equal—each a unique creation of God. The story of creation in the biblical book of Genesis records the formation of man from the dust of the earth and the breath of God. Then from the man's rib was created a helpmeet—a woman. Note that the woman was not formed from the head of the man, as if to rule over him, nor from the foot of the man, as if to be subjugated by him. Instead, the woman was formed from the side of the man, as if to walk beside the man as his life partner. Any other relationship does violence to the express purpose of creation.

Christian apostles urged men to give honor to their wives as the "weaker vessels," while at the same time recognizing the principle of headship of the husband as the spiritual leader of the family responsible to Jesus Himself.

In Christian marriage, the husband is expected to give himself to serve his wife in the same fashion that Christ gave Himself for the church. In that humble role of a servant, the husband is to love and cherish his wife in the same way that he would cherish his own body. The husband has the role of provider and protector of his wife and their children.

The wife in turn is a life partner. She is the one who gives stability to a family by supporting and encouraging her husband while she brings forth, nurtures, and disciplines the children.

During the 1960s and 1970s, "feminist" leaders taught young women that the biblical family model was a ruse perpetrated by what they called "the patriarchy." In their view, the traditional woman's role of wife and mother was little more than male-enforced slavery. Women were to be free of their stereotypical male-imposed bondage. Young women were taught that they had every right to compete with men in business, in the factories, in politics, and in the armed forces.

But what of the young women who longed for a traditional family, a protective caring husband, and children? In the outspoken views of the feminist culture, only career women could be accorded respect and status. The feminists wanted the sexes to be in conflict. To the feminists, traditional wives and mothers were weak and pitiful, living beneath their potential.

> *The woman was formed from the side of the man, as if to walk beside the man as his life partner.*

The bitter harvest of this nonsense was a generation of thoroughly confused, unhappy young women who often realized too late that the feminist poison had ruined their lives.

To be sure, the feminists were justified in rebelling against a system that denied women economic and social freedom. They rightfully protested the glass ceiling that limited advancement for women in business or the heavy doors that shut out their entrance into those preserves marked "For Men Only."

Unfortunately, a humble cry for equality soon degenerated into arrogance and hostility. Instead of skillful negotiation, there were bitter confrontations that allowed the most radical firebrands to take the lead while those advocating measured restraint were pushed into the background.

What are the consequences? The ancient prophet wrote, "For they sow the wind, and they shall reap the whirlwind."[2] Some forty years after the cultural revolution brought on by the feminists and their allies on the left, there have been over forty million abortions. The number of divorces exceeds the number of new marriages, and surveys indicate that the number of Americans of marriage age who prefer some type of long-term relationship other than marriage now exceeds 50 percent. Out-of-wedlock births have exploded, as has every known form of venereal disease (now called STDs, sexually transmitted diseases), from AIDS to genital warts and chlamydia. The fastest growing segment of the American poor is made up of single women with children.

> *During the 1960s and 1970s, "feminist" leaders taught young women that the biblical family model was a ruse perpetrated by what they called "the patriarchy."*

It is a sad fact that America now leads the world in every form of social pathology—alcoholism, drug abuse, juvenile delinquency, violent crime, family breakup, abortion, obesity, rates of incarceration. Obviously, all of this cannot be laid at the feet of radical feminism, but a large part can be charged to its account and its left-wing allies. There is no question that the radical left brought about in 1973 the widespread passage of so-called no-fault divorce legislation and the Supreme Court decision *Roe v. Wade*, which struck down state laws restricting abortion and declared for the first time in American history that a woman's desire to end the life of her unborn child was a "right" protected by the United States Constitution.

If stable, intact families and parental nurture of the young are indispensable pillars of an enduring civilization, then history will reveal that the pillars of our civilization are near collapse.

The lack of humility in feminism is obvious, but now our world is faced with male extremism as taught by the world's second largest religion, Islam. I recently completed the autobiographical account of the struggles of a Somali Muslim woman, Ayaan Hirsi Ali, titled *Infidel*. According to her, Muslim daughters and wives are mere chattel of fathers and husbands. For daughters, marriages are arranged by fathers. Often very young girls are married off to much older men. In the Muslim point of view, women are the source of male lust; therefore, they are to be not just veiled, but covered from head to foot so that no skin will be evident to tempt a male passerby.

According to the Koran, husbands are free to beat their wives. As to sexual relations, the Koran teaches that the wife is "your tillage, and you may enter your tillage as often as you like." Women who are raped are imprisoned for fornication. Women who are found guilty of adultery are beheaded. In court, a woman's testimony is accorded half the weight of the testimony of a man.

It is a sad fact that America now leads the world in every form of social pathology.

Miss Ali recorded the inability of Muslim women to travel, drive an automobile, or engage in normal business transactions without a male. In one Muslim country, she was denied access into the country from the airport until a male could come and take her into his custody.

Although in some Islamic countries the status of women has improved or is beginning to improve, it is an inescapable fact that in the preponderance of societies governed by the Koran and sharia law, women are regarded as less than men and are treated accordingly.

On the other hand, from the earliest days of the Judeo-Christian tradition, it is clear that women have been accorded some rights equal to those possessed by men. There is a clear insight into the property rights of unmarried women recorded in the book of Numbers, which was written as early as 1400 BC.

The lack of humility in feminism is obvious, but now our world is faced with male extremism as taught by the world's second largest religion, Islam.

It has been recorded that upon the death of a man named Zelophehad who had no male heir, a dispute arose concerning the inheritance rights of his unmarried daughters. The ruling made by Moses, ostensibly with God's concurrence, was that the daughters were free to take and hold an equal share of the inheritance with no hindrance whatsoever, so that their father's land would not be absorbed by some other relative. However, since the integrity of the grant of land to each tribe of Israel was considered of great importance, the unmarried daughters were not free to take their share of tribal land and marry outside their own tribe.

The case of the property rights of Zelophehad's daughters might well have become precedent for subsequent Jewish and Christian court decisions and legislation dealing with women's rights in what was obviously a most enlightened posture toward women's rights, considering the tribal customs of ancient history circa 1400 BC.

Returning to the present day, one aspect of the marriage relationship that should not involve pride is that of headship. Every organism or organization must have a head, some final source of authority. When Harry Truman was president of the United States, he had on his desk a little plaque stating simply, "The buck stops here." His office was the final authority in the federal executive branch. There was no other place to pass on responsibility. The president is the head. He has the authority and the responsibility.

Whether a family has two members or twenty, one of the partners must be the head.

Whether a family has two members or twenty, one of the partners must be the head. Normally, that person is the breadwinner and the husband. However, in today's world, women often have marketable skills that surpass those of many men, and, as a result, there is a role reversal. The wife becomes the head of the family, and the husband becomes a support person.

It doesn't take a genius to figure out what happens next. The husband feels emasculated and unsure of his identity. There easily can follow abuse of alcohol or drugs, extramarital sex, possible homosexuality, marital discord, and probably divorce. The successful career woman is devastated by her broken marriage and somehow can't understand what happened.

The normal order is for the husband to be the head of the family with the support and concurrence of his wife. Remember, it is the wife who makes him the head of the family after he shows her that he is willing to love and cherish her. It's not a question of pride for one person to have the final decision concerning vital family matters. If that person is the husband, then from the Christian perspective he is entitled to be the true head of the family only if he is committed to the will of God and God indeed is his head.

In my case, it is not only humility but common sense to recognize the unique wisdom and ability that God has given to my wife. We are life partners, and both of us need to be in agreement on important issues. She is a very accomplished interior decorator and designer, and she has an uncanny ability to read people. Not only that, she knows how to hear from the Lord. So we pray together about important and not-so-important issues.

Several years ago, the builder was finishing the massive Georgian-style headquarters building for the Christian Broadcasting Network. My wife and I hoped to find period antiques to use in several offices and public areas of the eighteenth-century-style building. One shopping trip was especially productive— beyond anything I could reasonably have expected. We found just what we needed at remarkable prices and left. After one more day of shopping in another location, I had experienced all the antique shopping I could stand and was ready to go home. The problem was, the new building and its companion were quite large, and we had only gotten half of what we needed.

I said to my wife, "I want to go home. What do you think?"

She said, "I'm not sure that would be wise."

So I said, "Let's pray about it and ask the Lord what to do."

So we prayed, and I asked the Lord, "What should we do?" The answer was crystal clear: "Listen to your wife."

So I asked her, "What did the Lord show you?" She smiled and said, "We should stay for at least two more days."

The head of the family had asked for direction from his authority who, in turn, referred him to his wife.

Humility said, "Your wife has a word from the Lord, so do as she says."

On those two extra days, there were auctions of what we needed at two leading auction houses, followed by a visit to a wholesale dealer I knew who had just received an incredible shipment. In two days we got exactly what we needed and filled a good-sized shipping container to send home. Over the past thirty years, the many guests visiting our headquarters have enjoyed the fruit of our journey. To add to our delight, the furniture has appreciated in value at least 500 percent since we bought it. Those extra two days were indeed a special blessing, all because my wife heard from the Lord and I humbled myself to respect His leading in her life. That is how biblical headship is supposed to work in marriage. Biblical headship is a wonderful partnership where two people love and respect each other. No fighting or dominance, only love and respect.

In my case, it is not only humility but common sense to recognize the unique wisdom and ability that God has given to my wife.

If only the feminists could realize the happiness that comes from marriage God's way!

So in conclusion, we say humility is the road to happiness and success in marriage, in business, in life.

Pride will always bring destruction. With God's help, we will contemplate humility and give ourselves to it.

LET THEM EAT CAKE

Pride grows in the human heart like lard on a pig.
ALEXANDER SOLZHENITSYN

As the revolutionary impulse against the eighteenth-century French monarchy and the self-indulgent French nobility was reaching a crescendo, food supplies were running out and the common people were starving. King Louis XVI was isolated from reality with his Austrian-born wife, Marie Antoinette. Theirs was a life of decadence and ease, filled with every conceivable luxury. Of course, they were proud because every day they were fawned over by servants, courtiers, and assorted sycophants.

Then a breathless messenger was given an audience with the king and queen. "Your Majesty," he said, "the people have no bread."

Bread was the staple of their diet. Bread is synonymous with food. In American slang, *bread* means money. Marie Antoinette knew nothing of the shortage. In the palace, there was always plenty of bread and an abundance of delicious cakes, petit fours, fruit tarts, rich pastries, and pies. She was not being malicious when she uttered the famous words, "Let them eat cake."

Louis and his wife were not vicious tyrants. They were not bloodthirsty warmongers. Instead, they were totally removed from the lives of their subjects. They were not humble servants of the people. They did not care for the poor and the needy. They did not concern themselves to create a nation where the citizens had justice under the rule of law, nor did they attempt to bring about a national economy under which there was prosperity and the people were able to meet their basic needs.

Theirs was a life of decadence and ease, filled with every conceivable luxury.

Instead, the monarchs concerned themselves with their clothes, their furnishings, their palaces and gardens, their hunts, their gambling, their banquets and soirees, their court attendants, and their guests. Every aspect of their lives fed pride and isolation. Every aspect of their lives served to alienate them from the people they should have humbly served.

History records the tragic tale of Marie Antoinette's being carried in a tumbrel through crowded streets to the guillotine where her head was severed from her body to the cheers of the bloodthirsty mob.

Slowly, inexorably, the biblical injunction will be worked out: "Pride goes before destruction, and a haughty spirit before a fall."[1]

Filled with pride, Nebuchadnezzar lost his mind and spent seven years living as an animal; Julius Caesar was stabbed to death; Alexander died far from home at age thirty-three; Queen Jezebel was hurled from a window and trampled to death by chariots; Cleopatra committed suicide by snakebite; Napoleon died in exile; Adolf Hitler committed suicide in a bunker in bombed-out Berlin; Mussolini was hanged in disgrace; the dictator of Romania, Ceausescu, was captured and shot. Following the 1929 stock market crash, a number of the proud captains of industry committed suicide or went to prison or took bankruptcy or in some other way faced disgrace. In the modern era, think of the fall of the once-proud leaders of Enron or Tyco or WorldCom. Dozens of proud, highly acclaimed corporate leaders did not get indicted and sent to prison; nevertheless, they were removed from their positions in a highly publicized fashion.

We are all cautioned to learn well the lessons of history. Pride will destroy the one who is ruled by it.

Yet humility will bring the one who chooses it a life filled with purpose and blessing.

How then do we obtain humility and avoid pride? I would offer for your consideration six rules of conduct to put your life in its proper place.

1. *Always acknowledge the greatness and power of almighty God.* Recognize that you are nothing more than a speck inside a vast universe. However wise, strong, talented, beautiful, appealing, or rich you may be, these attributes are laughably small in light of God's majesty, His wisdom, and His everlasting riches in glory.

True humility begins with a frank appraisal of your abilities and failings in comparison to His perfection.

2. *Avoid personal praise like the plague.* Remember, the genes that form you were in place from your grandparents. How then can you be proud of inherited ability? Deflect the praise from yourself and give it to God, your parents, your ancestors, your teachers, your coaches, your spouse, your fellow workers.

The story is told of the great nineteenth-century preacher D. L. Moody, who was met by two ladies as he was coming out of the hall where he had been speaking.

"Oh, Mr. Moody, that was the most wonderful message we have ever heard," they crooned.

Moody stopped and stared at them. "What are you ladies trying to do, ruin my ministry?"

To Moody, the problem was obvious. If ever he stopped thinking of Jesus Christ and began to focus on his own oratorical ability, his ministry would have ceased. Therefore, he immediately deflected the seemingly well-meant compliment because he realized the insidious danger of pride.

> *Humility will bring the one who chooses it a life filled with purpose and blessing.*

To those of us who deal with our fellowmen a bit less harshly when we are given a compliment, the answer is a simple "Thank you. I praise God that He blessed." However it is done, always deflect praise from you and give it to Him.

3. *Form in your own mind a clear and honest appraisal of yourself and your abilities.* One of the most popular programs on U.S. television is a talent contest called *American Idol*. Leading up

to the final episodes is a parade of singers, many of whom are embarrassingly bad. They should not be singing in the shower much less on national television, and yet they are willing to suffer humiliation for the privilege of appearing on television.

Just as some singers do not have the ability to take on public performances, even so some people with mechanical ability should try a trade school rather than a four-year college. Some athletes who perform well in high school will never have the physical ability to compete against professionals. A C-average student in high school with an IQ of 120 will not succeed against geniuses at MIT. Yet there are brilliant singers, athletes, scholars, writers, and planners who just need an opportunity to succeed. We should never sell ourselves short, but if we attempt feats that totally exceed our innate abilities, we will be doomed to frustration and despair.

Always deflect praise from you and give it to Him.

We are told in the Bible to regard ourselves soberly. If we have great ability, we are to humbly exercise that ability and give God credit for it. We should strive to the limit of our natural abilities, and yet always be prepared to give our Creator thanks and glory for the life within us that makes any achievement possible.

4. *The road to humility leads us to magnify the excellence of others*. In marriage, each spouse must constantly seek out and admire the excellent qualities of his or her partner.

In sports, the humble person is always willing to praise and congratulate a teammate or an opponent. In work, there should be sincere appreciation and gratitude for the contributions of superiors, subordinates, and fellow workers. Note the word *sincere*. Not grudging and false, but sincere appreciation.

There are few things more guaranteed to create resentment in a work environment than a superior who appropriates the plans and concepts of subordinates and then attempts to take credit for them himself. The humble person, as the saying goes, "feels comfortable in his own skin," so he has no reluctance to share praise or rewards with others.

5. *As much as we may dislike it, the path to humility leads through honest helpful criticism, malicious criticism, and encounters with mean-spirited people*. The beauty of diamonds and precious stones and the luster of wood are brought out only by rough, seemingly cruel abrasion. There is the saw, the grinding wheel, and the planing

tool, increasingly fine levels of abrasion, all of which slowly but surely bring forth a beautiful luster and radiance.

We should be willing to embrace the rough places in life and the sorrows, griefs, and tragedies that come to us all, knowing that these are God's tools in this process of making us humble servants of God and man.

6. *Realizing that "God opposes the proud but favors the humble,"[2] each day we must consciously do two things.* We must first remind ourselves of our own mortality. We have seventy years, in some cases eighty or even ninety. But then life leaves our bodies, and our bodies are placed in the dirt. A sports career lasts less than ten years. Youthful beauty lasts perhaps twenty years. A business or professional career usually lasts thirty to thirty-five years. A high-level political career can be as short as four or as long as forty years. However long they may be, all life's callings end, and each of us moves off the stage while someone else takes our place.

Again, to paraphrase Moses, "Let us contemplate death that we may be wise."[3]

We must also humble ourselves daily. Diligently seek humility. Earnestly ask God for humility. Consciously deflate your own ego. Always look for opportunities during your brief life span to serve others. Follow the steps that can lead to realizing in your life *the greatest virtue*. I close with these words from the apostle Peter: "All of you, serve each other in humility, for 'God opposes the proud but favors the humble.' So humble yourselves under the mighty power of God, and at the right time he will lift you up in honor."[4]

We should never sell ourselves short, but if we attempt feats that totally exceed our innate abilities, we will be doomed to frustration and despair.

*The proud man counts his newspaper
clippings—the humble man his blessings.*

FULTON J. SHEEN

NOTES

Foreword

1. The Torah prohibits Jews from destroying or erasing the Hebrew name of God: "And you shall destroy their names from this place. Do not do this to Adonai, your God" (Deuteronomy 12:3-4). It is a sign of respect for Jews to spell God's name with a hyphen, G-d, and avoid the possibility of accidentally erasing His name.

2. Micah 6:8 NKJV

Chapter 2: Corrupted by Beauty

1. Isaiah 14:12-14 NKJV
2. Ezekiel 28:13-17 ESV
3. Proverbs 16:18 NIV
4. Luke 12:15 NKJV
5. Luke 16:15 NIV
6. James 4:1-2, 6 NLT

Chapter 3: "One Who Serves"

1. Philippians 2:6-10 NLT
2. Isaiah 14:13 ESV
3. Proverbs 22:4 NKJV
4. 1 Peter 5:5 NKJV
5. Numbers 12:7 NKJV
6. Numbers 12:3 NIV

Chapter 4: Relative Strength

1. Psalm 139:14 NKJV
2. Psalm 8:3-4 ESV
3. Psalm 111:10 NIV
4. Galatians 6:14 NKJV

Chapter 5: A Messenger of Satan

1. 2 Corinthians 12:2 NIV
2. 2 Corinthians 12:7 NKJV
3. 1 Corinthians 4:13 NKJV
4. 2 Corinthians 12:7 NKJV
5. 2 Corinthians 12:7 NKJV
6. Joel 3:2 NIV
7. Psalm 90:12 NLT

Chapter 7: Like a Little Child

1. Mark 10:45 ESV
2. Matthew 18:3 NIV
3. Proverbs 3:5-6 NLT
4. Proverbs 3:6 NLT

Chapter 8: One Flesh

1. Genesis 2:24 NKJV
2. Hosea 8:7 ESV

Chapter 9: Let Them Eat Cake

1. Proverbs 16:18 NKJV
2. James 4:6 NLT
3. Psalm 90:12, paraphrase
4. 1 Peter 5:5-6 NLT